Tuning Your Guitar

Check the tuning of your guitar every time you pick it up. What you play will sound better and the tuning process will help to develop your 'ear' or sense of pitch.

The easiest way to tune your strings is to match them with the guitar strings played on the CD (if you have bought the book & CD version). Many players use electronic tuners which check the pitch of each string. Another possibility is to use 'relative tuning' after one string has been tuned correctly.

Relative Tuning

Check the pitch of the 1st string by comparing it to an electronic keyboard or tuning fork. The open 1st string (i.e. with no finger on it) should be an **e** note. If you have an **a** tuning fork, the 5th fret note should match the pitch produced by the fork. Tighten or loosen the string gradually until the pitch of the string is correct. When the 1st string is the right pitch, follow these steps to tune the other strings in relation to it:

Tune your 2nd string to the 1st string. Put your left hand finger on the 5th fret of the 2nd string and play the note with the right hand or flatpick. Now play the open 1st string. These two notes should be the same. Tighten the 2nd string if it's too low in pitch and loosen it if it's too high.

Tune your 3rd string to the open 2nd string. This time press the 4th fret of the 3rd string down and sound the note. It should be the same as the open 2nd string. *Tune the 4th to the open 3rd, the 5th to the open 4th and the 6th to the open 5th* by comparing the 5th fret note on the lower string to the pitch of the string above.

The diagram below shows the first five frets of the guitar fingerboard and where you should put your finger for tuning each string relative to the next:

Strings

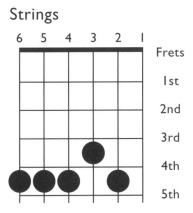

Your First Chord: A Major

Hold your guitar as shown on the previous page, and finger an **A** chord. The diagram below is a chord 'window,' showing the end of the fingerboard (imagine the guitar neck pointing to the sky). Thus the strings are going down the page. The numbers in circles tell you which finger to use. Your index finger is 1, middle 2, ring 3 and little one 4.

The picture below shows you how the chord should look. All 3 fingers are on the same fret (the second fret) so twist your hand to the left slightly. Try to have a slight gap between the neck of the guitar and your hand.

A Chord

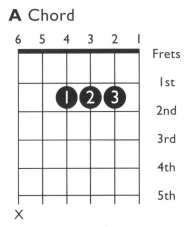

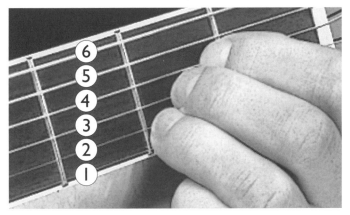

Press all 3 fingers down firmly, with your thumb about midway on the back of the neck, and play each string (start with the 5th string, A) with your right hand thumb, or flatpick. The 5th and 1st strings are played 'open' i.e. with no finger on them. The **X** underneath the 6th string means 'don't play this string.' Play each string slowly, one by one, and move your finger or hand to stop any buzzing. Make sure you have a 'clean' sound now. Good.

Let's have a look at two more chords so you can play your first song...

Useful Information

3

Mull Of Kintyre

Wings

Strumming Style

D and E Chords

Hundreds of songs can be played with just three chords. The two other chords that are usually found with the **A** chord are the **D** and **E** chords...

D Chord

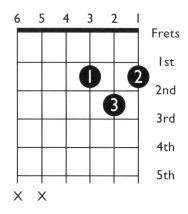

6	5	4	3	2	1	
						Frets
			①		②	1st
				③		2nd
						3rd
						4th
						5th
X	X					

E Chord

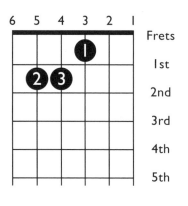

6	5	4	3	2	1	
			①			Frets
						1st
	②	③				2nd
						3rd
						4th
						5th

Hold each chord as shown and play the strings one at a time (for the **D** chord, don't play the 6th or 5th strings). If you get buzzing noises, here are some possible reasons:

You're not pressing down on the strings hard enough. Your nails may be too long.

The back of another finger is getting in the way. Or your hand is touching the 1st string. Try to adjust your fingers and hand so the top of the finger is more vertical (not so flat).

Your finger is not close enough to the metal strip (fretwire) in front of it. The further from the strip your finger is, the harder you'll have to press to avoid buzzing. With some chords, like **A**, you can't always get every finger close to it, but try to get as close as you can.

When you can play all three chords cleanly, you're ready to try your first strum.

Your First Strum

Finger an **A** chord. Holding them together, brush down with the backs of your right hand fingers across the strings from 5th to 1st (bass to treble). Extend the fingers as your hand moves downwards. Now try this simple rhythm:

3/4 Rhythm

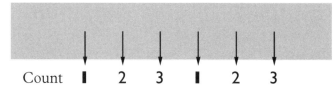

Count   **1**   2   3   **1**   2   3

The arrows indicate downward strums. Count each group '1 2 3,' as shown, keeping the beats evenly spaced. The first strum of three is stressed by playing it louder. This creates the 3/4 rhythm.

Now try the same rhythm pattern with the **D** and **E** chords. Keep the pace quite slow for the moment. Finally, try to change chords with the left hand while keeping the rhythm steady with the right. Once you can do this try the accompaniment on the next page.

Don't try to go too fast, otherwise you'll have to stop to change chords, and it might be hard to change the habit.

The Complete Guitar Player

by Russ Shipton

Book 1

Amsco Publications London / New York / Paris / Sydney / Copenhagen / Madrid / Tokyo

Your Guitar

Machine Heads
(Tuning Pegs)

Nut

Frets

Fingerboard

Neck

Sound Hole

Table (Face)

Bridge Saddle

Body

Bridge

The Capo

It would be very useful for you to have a 'capo.'
This device helps you to make the level of playing
(the pitch of the notes) suit the range of the voice.
The capo is illustrated and discussed on the
pull-out chart.

The Flatpick

You might prefer to use a flatpick for the
strumming and bass-strum styles as it will save your
fingernails from wearing down and help you to
produce more volume.

Holding Your Guitar

When playing modern guitar styles, this is the
way you can hold your guitar:

The Right Hand

When strumming with the fingers, hold them
close together. For picking styles, put the wrist out
to the front slightly and keep the thumb a little to
the left of the fingers. The index, middle and ring
fingers are held over the three treble strings.

When strumming with a flatpick, hold it firmly
between the thumb and side of the index finger.

The Left Hand

The fingertips press the strings down.
The palm of the hand should be kept clear of the
neck. The thumb should be behind the 1st and
2nd fingers, midway on the neck for a good grip
and free movement.

General

The crook of your arm should grip the 'corner'
of the guitar body. Then your right hand should
fall over the rear half of the sound hole. Try not to
have a cramped position. Both hands should be
clear of the guitar, giving the fingers room to move.

Accompaniment: 3/4 Rhythm

Chorus

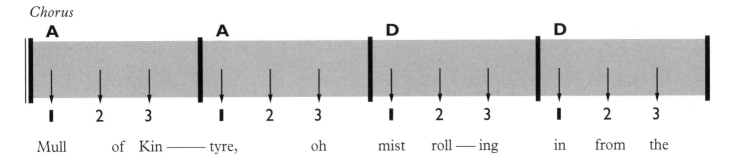

Mull   of   Kin——tyre,   oh   mist   roll——ing   in   from   the

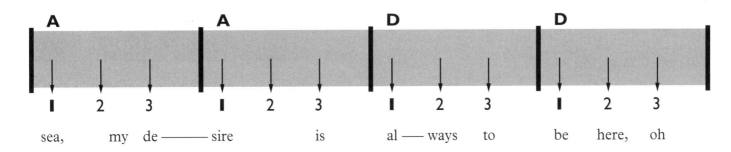

sea,   my   de———sire   is   al——ways   to   be   here,   oh

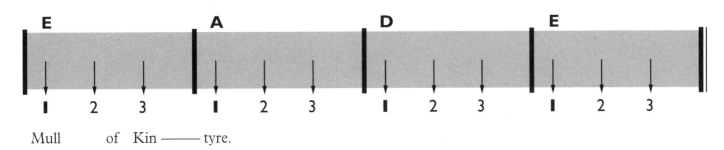

Mull   of   Kin——tyre.

Strumming Style

 Notes

Bar Lines: *Separate the groups of 3 strums. The 1st beat/strum in each bar is the heavy one.*

Length Of Strums: *Don't try to hit all the strings on every strum. Perhaps you can start by hitting 5 or 6 strings for the heavy strum, and 3 or 4 strings on the others.*

Using The Flatpick: *Instead of using your right hand fingers, you might prefer using a flatpick. Keep it angled slightly so it glides across the strings. Whether you use your fingers or flatpick, don't hit the strings too hard!*

Singing: *When you're able to change chords smoothly and play through the accompaniment at a moderate pace, try singing the chorus words as shown. The first melody note is the 2nd fret of the 4th string.*

Verse: *The verse chords are shown with the other lyrics at the end of the book.*

Words and Music by McCartney-Laine

The Times They Are A-Changin'

Bob Dylan

Strumming Style

Chord Changing

The **A**, **D** & **E** chords are used again for this song. Can you remember them without looking at the diagrams? The sooner you remember the chords, the quicker you'll progress.

If you're having trouble changing chords, try putting your 1st finger down first, and the others just after. In no time you'll find you can put them all down together!

Take all accompaniments slowly to start with, and then you won't have to stop or slow down to get into the next chord position. When you can play the whole song slowly, try speeding up to the correct tempo.

Singing

Most people find singing a little strange at first, but almost everybody is able to pitch their voice correctly to make a reasonable sound. So persevere, even if you feel a little awkward now. I've made the timing of the singing a little easier to follow than the original songs in many cases. When you're in complete control of the playing side of things, time the words as you feel fit. It would help your general progress if you committed the 1st verse (and chorus where appropriate) to memory.

Upstrums

Now you've got the simple 3/4 strum pattern mastered, let's complicate things with upstrums. As your fingers come up to be ready for the next downstrum, they can strike some treble strings on the way. These upstrums are off the beat and not so 'important' as the downstrums, so they can be hit more lightly. Only two or three treble strings need be played.

If you want to use a flatpick, turn your wrist to angle the pick the other way for the upstrums:

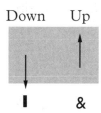

Hold an **A** chord and play a downstrum followed by an upstrum:

Now play several in a row:

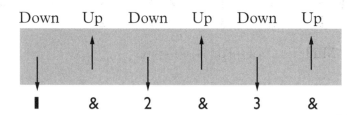

Make sure the upstrums are exactly halfway between the downstrums. Patterns often involve just one or two upstrums. In 'The Times They Are A-Changin', the first pattern has one upstrum. Count it: 1 2 & 3. The other pattern has two upstrums and is counted: 1 & 2 & 3. Play the accompaniment with just the first pattern, then with just the second pattern.

Finally, alternate the patterns as shown. It's a lot to remember, especially while singing, but it's worth the effort!

| | = Strum down |
| | = Strum up |

Accompaniment: 3/4 Rhythm

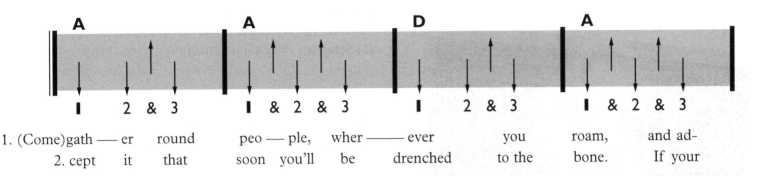

1. (Come)gath ——— er   round   peo —— ple,   wher ——— ever   you   roam,   and ad-
2. cept   it   that   soon you'll   be   drenched   to the   bone.   If your

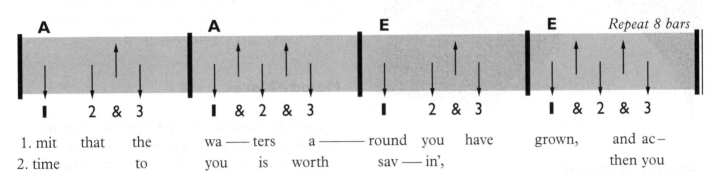

Repeat 8 bars

1. mit   that   the   wa —— ters   a ——— round   you   have   grown,   and ac—
2. time   to   you   is   worth   sav —— in',   then you

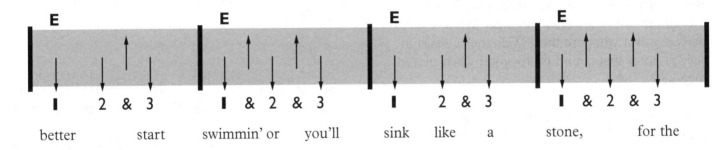

better   start   swimmin' or   you'll   sink   like   a   stone,   for the

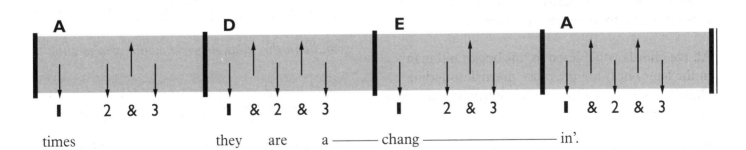

times   they   are   a ——— chang ——————————— in'.

(Notes)

Speed: *Play the accompaniment slowly at first. Keep the beats evenly spaced and the rhythm as steady as possible. Repeat the first 8 bars with the second line of lyrics.*

Extra Bars: *As Bob Dylan often does, add one or more bars of* **A** *at the end of the sequence, before singing the second verse.*

Melody Notes: *Singing this song is easy at the start - the 2nd fret note of the 3rd string is used for every syllable of 'Come gather round people.'*

Strumming Style

Words and Music by Bob Dylan
Copyright © 1963 & 1964 by Warner Brothers Inc.; renewed 1991, 1992 Special Rider Music.
All Rights Reserved. International Copyright Secured.

7

Candle In The Wind

Elton John & Bernie Taupin

Strumming Style

What's A Chord?

We're staying with the same three chords for this and the next song, so you'll get to know them perfectly. But what are they? Well, they consist of several notes that sound pretty good when played together.

Count the notes in each chord - you should find 6 for **E**, 5 for **A**, and 4 for **D**. But though in a way you're right, some notes are similar enough to be given the same name (these are said to be octaves of each other). So basically these chords have three notes in them, though some are repeated.

All the chords you'll learn in this book (and many in the later ones) are the most 'normal' sounding chords. Some are called 'major' chords; like the ones you've learned so far.

Below I've shown another rhythm for you to try, and now you know the **A**, **D** and **E** chords quite well (see if you can stop looking at your left hand— even when it changes chords). Then you can concentrate on what your right hand is doing. It's very important to get a steady rhythm. You'll also have time to give some attention to your singing.

Another Rhythm

The most common rhythm in modern music is 4/4. If the first number indicates the number of beats, what do you think the basic strumming pattern for this rhythm will be? Yes, you've guessed it. A heavy strum followed by three lighter ones. Let's try it...

4/4 Rhythm Hold any chord

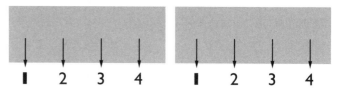

Count **1** 2 3 4, **1** 2 3 4, etc. Stress the first beat strum and follow with three lighter strums. Keep the strums evenly spaced, as before.

Melody Notes

The melody notes are usually the notes that are sung. You could also try playing the single notes while a friend plays the chorus accompaniment as shown. Or you could record yourself playing the chords, then play the melody along with the recording.

String	⌐2nd⌐	⌐—1st—⌐	2nd	⌐—1st—⌐	⌐2nd⌐
Fret	2 3 0	0 0 2	0	0 0 2	3

And it seems to me you lived your life like a

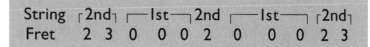

⌐—1st—⌐ 3rd ⌐2nd⌐ ⌐———1st———⌐
0 0 0 2 2 2 3 0 0 0 0 2 0

candle in the wind, never knowing who to cling to

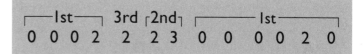

⌐———2nd———⌐ ⌐———1st———⌐
3 2 2 0 0 0 0 2 2 2 4

when the rain set in. And I would have liked to

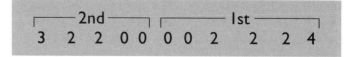

⌐———1st———⌐3rd2nd3rd ⌐2nd⌐
4 5 4 4 2 0 2 2 2 2 2 2

have known you, but I was just a kid. Your candle

2nd 1st ⌐2nd⌐ ⌐4th⌐ ⌐3rd⌐2nd4th
3 0 2 0 0 2 4 2 2 0 4

burnt out long before your legend ever did.

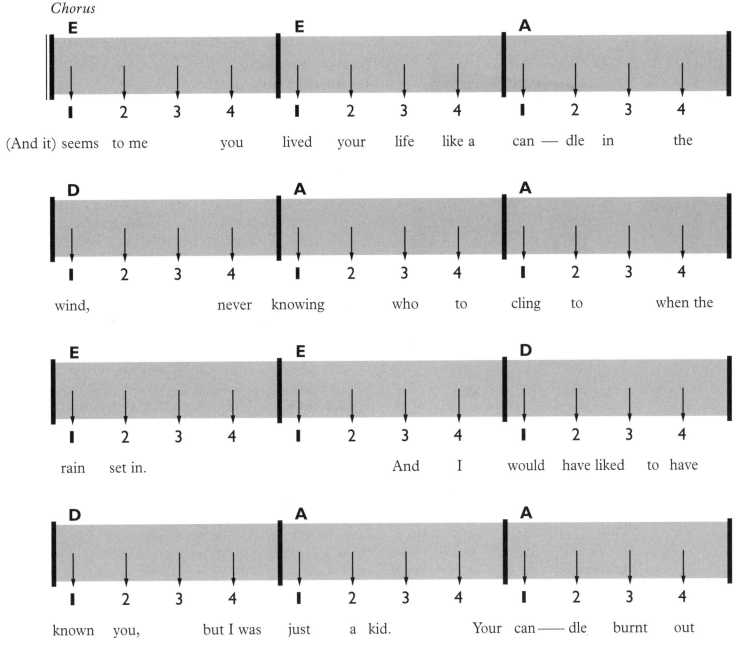

Accompaniment: 4/4 Rhythm

= Strum down

Chorus

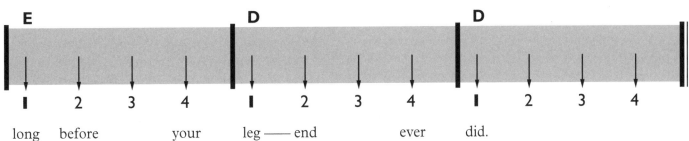

Singing: *Sing 'And it' before starting the accompaniment for the chorus shown above.*

Verse: *The verse chords are shown with the other lyrics at the end of the book.*

Ending: *The last chord shown is a* **D**, *but you can add a bar of* **A** *and a bar of* **E** *before singing the verse. Finish the song with an* **A** *chord strum after the two bars of* **D**.

Strumming Style

Words & Music by Elton John & Bernie Taupin

Blowin' In The Wind

Bob Dylan

Upstrums

As we did with the 3/4 rhythm, let's add some upstrums to the simple 4/4 pattern, and make things sound a bit more interesting. Finger an **E** chord and try these patterns:

4/4 Rhythm

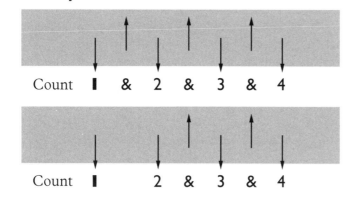

Accompaniment: 4/4 Rhythm

Notice the extra upstrum in the last bar of both verse and chorus. Don't forget to keep a steady rhythm (and slow to start with), with each downstrum equally spaced whether or not there's an upstrum before or after it.

Melody Notes

Singing the first note of a song is not always easy. Find out which note in the chord is the one you sing for the first word (occasionally it's not a note in the chord that I show first but that doesn't matter). It makes for a much stronger beginning if you know exactly what note you're about to sing!

The first note of 'Blowin' In The Wind' (for 'How') is found on the 2nd fret of the 4th string, or the open 1st string for high voices. As a change to playing the normal accompaniment, try playing the melody while a friend plays the chorus. Here are the notes of the chorus, with the string and fret shown, as before:

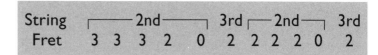

String		2nd				3rd	2nd			3rd
Fret	3	3	3	2	0	2	2	2	0	2

The answer, my friend, is blowin' in the wind

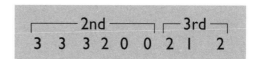

	2nd				3rd	
3	3	3	2	0	0	2	1	2

The answer is blowin' in the wind.

Lyrics

In most cases the words of the 1st verse are shown beneath the notation. When parts of the song are very similar, later words are put under the same bars of notation. This gives you less to remember. Soon you'll be using many slight variations to make your guitar accompaniments more interesting.

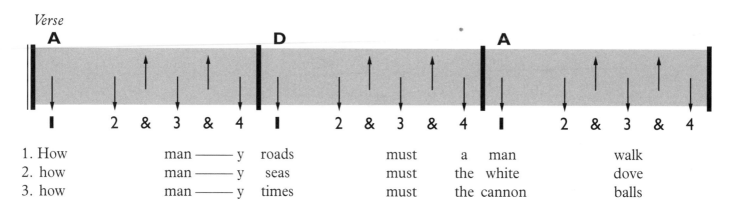

	= Strum down
	= Strum up

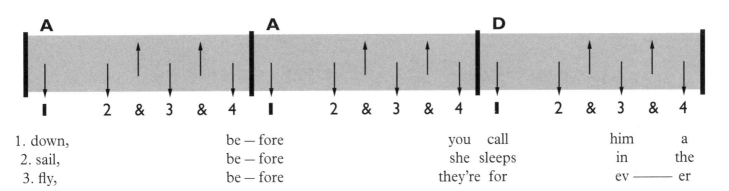

A   **A**   **D**

1. down,   be — fore   you call   him   a
2. sail,   be — fore   she sleeps   in   the
3. fly,   be — fore   they're for   ev ——— er

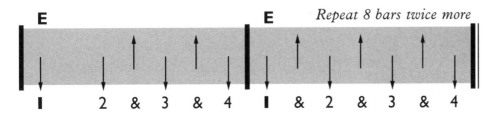

E   **E**   *Repeat 8 bars twice more*

1. man?   Yes'n
2. sand?   The
3. banned?

Chorus

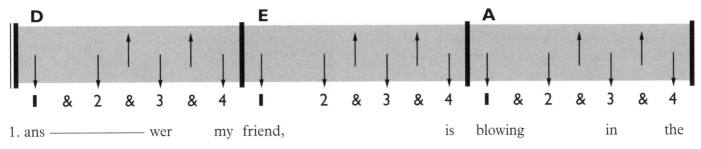

D   **E**   **A**

1. ans ————— wer   my friend,   is blowing   in   the

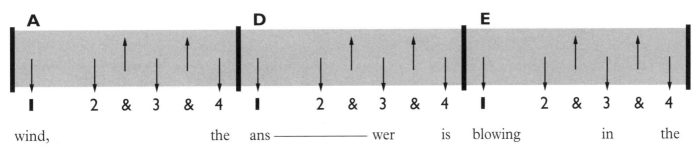

A   **D**   **E**

wind,   the ans ————— wer is blowing   in   the

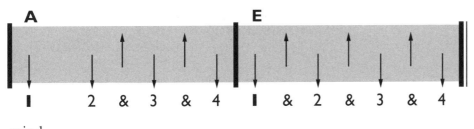

A   **E**

wind.

Hey Jude

The Beatles

Strumming Style

Downstrums Between Beats

Another kind of rhythmic feel is created when *downstrums* are played between beats instead of upstrums. This sort of rhythm pattern often suits slow ballads:

4/4 Rhythm Hold any chord

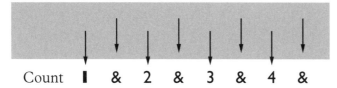

Count **I** & 2 & 3 & 4 &

Make the downstrums between the beats shorter than those on the beats, across two or three lower strings. Stress the 1st beat strum more than the others, but to get the correct rhythmic feel you must do a full strum on each beat and *stress all the beats reasonably heavily*. This will produce more of a 'plodding' rhythm. The strums between beats must again be played exactly halfway between.

As with the previous strum patterns, some strums between beats can be removed to create different patterns. Try this variation:

4/4 Rhythm Hold any chord

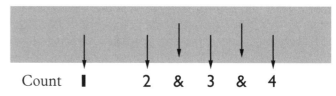

Count **I**   2 & 3 & 4

E7 Chord

So far you've used the **A**, **D** and **E** chords only. These are simple major chords involving three notes. When **A** is the main chord, you could try using an **E7** (**E** seventh) chord instead of **E**. This creates a stronger 'pull' back to the **A** chord and provides more variety. 7 chords have four notes, one more than the ordinary major chord. Here are two easy ways of holding an **E7** chord:

E7 Chord

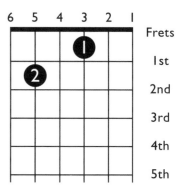

E7 Chord

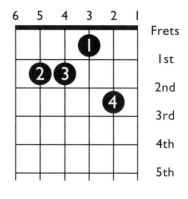

The extra note is an octave higher in the second **E7** shown. Try both shapes in the accompaniment for 'Hey Jude.'

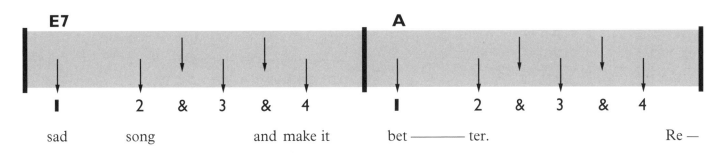

= Strum down

Accompaniment: 4/4 Rhythm

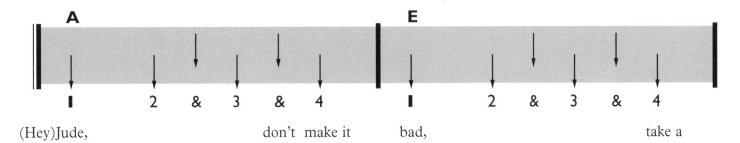

A

| 1 | 2 | & | 3 | & | 4 |

(Hey)Jude,   don't make it

E

| 1 | 2 | & | 3 | & | 4 |

bad,   take a

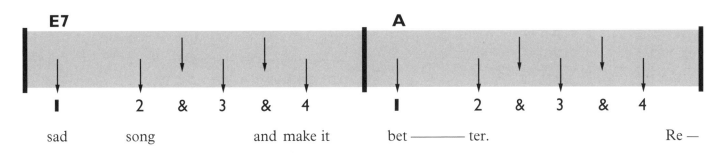

E7

| 1 | 2 | & | 3 | & | 4 |

sad   song   and make it

A

| 1 | 2 | & | 3 | & | 4 |

bet ——— ter.   Re —

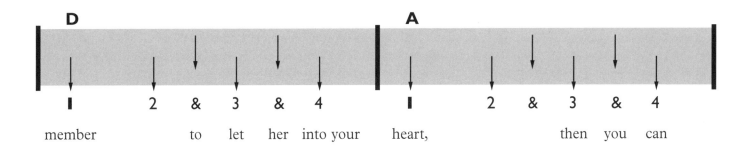

D

| 1 | 2 | & | 3 | & | 4 |

member   to   let   her   into your

A

| 1 | 2 | & | 3 | & | 4 |

heart,   then   you   can

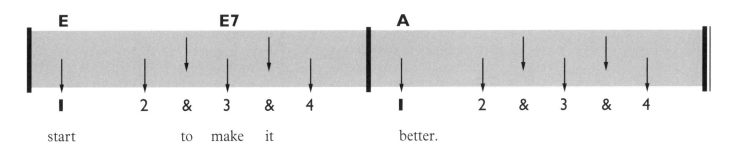

E   **E7**

| 1 | 2 | & | 3 | & | 4 |

start   to   make   it

A

| 1 | 2 | & | 3 | & | 4 |

better.

Notes

Middle Section: *The chords for the middle section of 'Hey Jude' are given with the other lyrics at the end of the book.*

Melody: *The first two notes of the tune are the open 1st string and 2nd fret of the 2nd string.*

Mid-Bar Chord Change: *Notice the chord change in the seventh bar. Add your little finger or remove the 3rd finger on the 3rd beat of the bar.*

Summary

Strum Patterns

Here are the 3/4 and 4/4 strum patterns you've already seen, plus a few more...

3/4 Rhythm

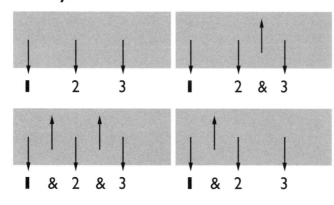

4/4 Rhythm

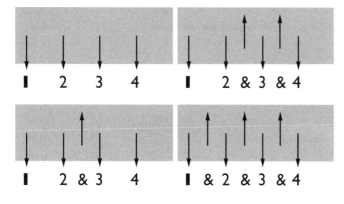

4/4 Rhythm *(with downstrums between beats)*

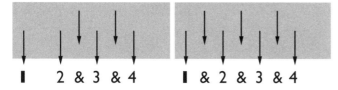

Play each of the patterns over and over until you can play them smoothly at different speeds. Experiment with putting different patterns together in an accompaniment.

You could also create some patterns of your own by varying the number of offbeat strums. An upstrum might be added at the end of a pattern when the same chord is used for the following bar.

With an upstroke at the end, the second 3/4 pattern would be counted: **❙ 2 & 3** &. Then you'd go straight into the first beat or downstrum of the next bar. Putting an upstroke at the end of the second 4/4 pattern, it would be counted: **❙ 2 & 3 & 4** &.

Other Songs

Here is a list of other songs that you can play with *just three chords:*

3/4
A Hard Rain's A-Gonna Fall
The Happy Birthday Song
Lucille
The Wild Rover
There Goes My Everything
Irene Goodnight
Amazing Grace

4/4
(I Can't Get No) Satisfaction
It's Only Rock 'N Roll (But I Like It)
Leaving On A Jet Plane
C'mon Everybody
Three Steps To Heaven
The Sloop John B.
Rave On
Heartbeat
Bad Moon Rising
Save The Last Dance For Me
Last Thing On My Mind
Ob-La-Di, Ob-La-Da
I Feel Fine
The Ballad Of John And Yoko

4/4 *(with downstrums between beats)*
Let It Be
Get Back
I Still Haven't Found What I'm Looking For
Brimful Of Asha
Father And Son
Knockin' On Heaven's Door
The Joker

How To Do It

The bass-strum style is halfway between strumming and finger-picking. Your thumb strikes individual strings, and the fingers brush across the treble strings. Normally the strums are shorter than in ordinary strumming.

Let's have a look at the simple 3/4 and 4/4 patterns...

3/4 Rhythm Finger an **A** Chord

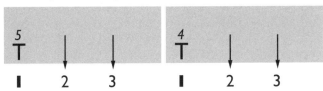

4/4 Rhythm Finger an **E** Chord

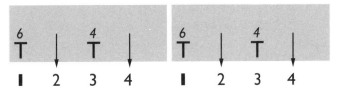

As you've guessed, the 'T's mean the thumb strikes. The number on top of the T means the string your thumb has to hit. In the patterns shown above, the thumb strike replaces a downstrum on the first beat of every bar in the 3/4 rhythm. In the 4/4 bars, two downstrums are replaced by thumb strikes: the first and the third.

Count the bars as usual, keeping a steady rhythm. Don't move your right hand too much, or your thumb won't be in the right position for the next bass string strike.

Using A Flatpick

Many players use a flatpick for the bass-strum style instead of thumb and fingers. If you used a pick for the strumming style, you could also try it for this style too. Strike the individual string that is indicated above the 'T' in the notation.

Use a downward motion and keep the right hand quite close to the strings to help you hit the correct bass string.

Now you're ready for some more great songs!

Simple 4/4 Pattern Sequence
Finger an **E** chord

Thumb strikes 6th string

Strum down

Thumb strikes 4th string

Strum down

Catch The Wind

Donovan

Bass-Strum Style

A7 and G Chords

When a song starts and ends with an **A** chord, it will have been played 'in the key of **A**.' The two other chords usually found with the **A** chord are the **D** and **E** chords, as you've seen. When a song starts and ends with the **D** chord, the key will be **D**, and the other two chords generally found with the **D** chord will be the **A** and **G** chords.

You already know the **A** chord, but quite often, when moving to the **D** chord, the **A7** will be used. So let's have a look at the **A7** and the **G** chords.

A7 Chord

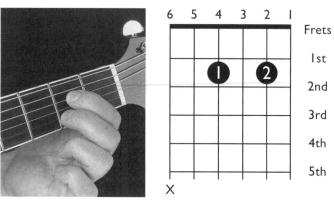

G Chord

The **A7** can also be fingered with the 2nd and 3rd fingers. If you find it easier, for the moment you could use the 4th finger instead of the 3rd for the **G** chord. Keep the left hand thumb on the middle of the back of the neck.

Upstrokes

The accompaniment involves two alternating bass-strum patterns, one with no upstrums, and the other with a single upstrum. To start with, you could use just the first pattern throughout, then the second pattern throughout, then finally play both as shown.

Melody Notes

Here are the notes of 'Catch The Wind' to help you sing the melody correctly. You could also play them on the guitar along with the accompaniment (played on CD or by a friend).

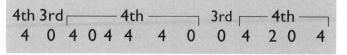

String	3rd											4th
Fret	2 2 2 2	2		2	2	2	2	2 2 0	4

In the chilly hours and minutes of uncertainty,

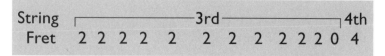

4th 3rd	4th		3rd	4th
4 0 4 0 4 4	4	0	0 4	2 0 4

I want to be in the warm hold of your lovin' mind.

The second half of the verse has a similar melody, but ends on a **D** note.

Accompaniment: 3/4 Rhythm

$\frac{4}{T}$	= Thumb plays 4th string
↓	= Strum down
↑	= Strum up

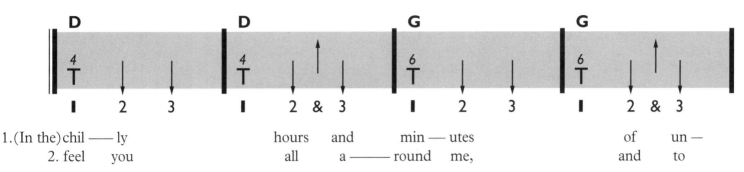

1. (In the) chil —— ly   hours and min —— utes   of un —
2. feel you   all a —— round me,   and to

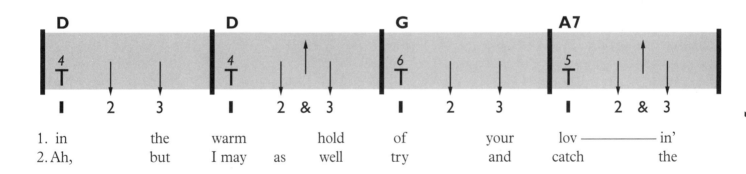

1. cert — ain — ty,   I want to be
2. take your hand a —— long the sand.

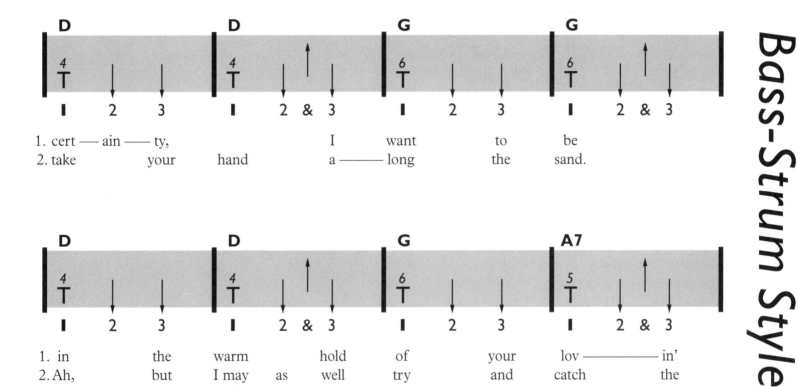

1. in the warm hold of your lov ———— in'
2. Ah, but I may as well try and catch the

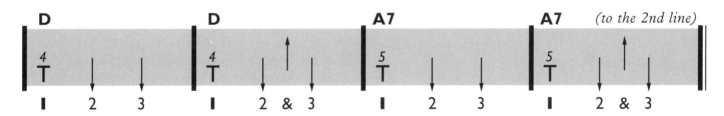

(to the 2nd line)

1. mind,
2. wind!

 Notes

Speed: *As usual play the accompaniment slowly at first. When you can remember the sequence, try singing the top line of words. The 2nd half of the verse has the same chord sequence.*

Bass Notes: *When two bars in a row involve the same chord, you can strike a different bass string. Try striking the 5th string in bars 2, 4, 6 & 10 for a more varied sound.*

Mr. Tambourine Man

Bob Dylan

Bass-Strum Style

'Clean Playing'

This is a reminder to those of you who may be blindly (or is it deafly?) bashing away, without really listening to the sort of sounds you and your guitar are producing. Can you answer 'Yes' to these three questions?

Are you tuning your guitar every time you pick it up?
If it's not in tune, however well you follow my directions, the overall sound won't be very nice to listen to.

Are you pressing down hard enough on the strings?
However well you do with your rhythm, it's your left hand that determines the quality of the sound that comes out. Try to practice a little each day and the ends of your fingers will harden up. Then you'll find it easier to press down.

Are your left hand finger nails very short?
Cut them regularly and that'll help you press down on the strings properly. Don't let your fingers get too far from the metal strip (fret wire) either, and that'll help you get a 'clean' sound. If you concentrate for a couple of weeks on producing pure sounds, with little or no buzzing noises, after that you'll soon do it automatically. This is a good time to get rid of any bad habits!

Using The Capo

In my 'useful information' notes at the start of the book, I mentioned the capo. If you find the melody of a song too low for you to sing comfortably, try using your capo.

In the picture below, a **D** chord (shape) is fingered, but with a capo placed on the third fret. The capo effectively shortens the neck of the guitar and increases the pitch of all the strings by the same amount. This means that the capo can be treated as the end of the neck (i.e. as the 'nut') and the same shapes can be fingered.

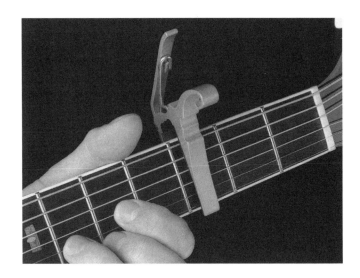

Bass Notes

For the **D** chord (and sometimes the **G**), I've given the 3rd string as a 'bass string' strike. Though the 6th, 5th and 4th strings are generally considered to be the bass strings and the other three the treble, in this and other picking styles the 3rd is often picked out by the thumb or pick.

After striking the 3rd string you can still hit it along with the others for the strums following.

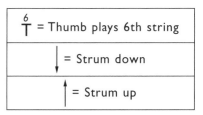

Accompaniment: 4/4 Rhythm

Chorus

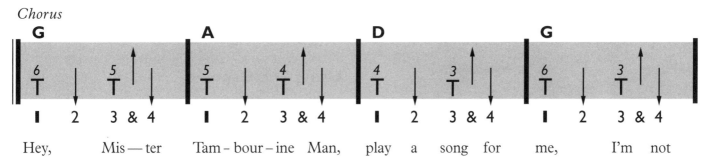

Hey,   Mis — ter   Tam - bour – ine   Man,   play   a   song   for   me,   I'm   not

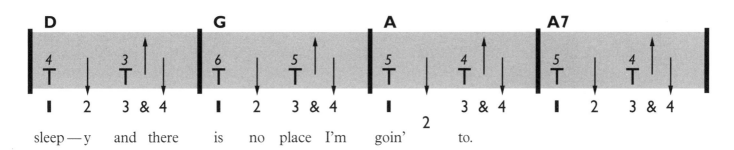

sleep — y   and   there   is   no   place   I'm   goin'   to.

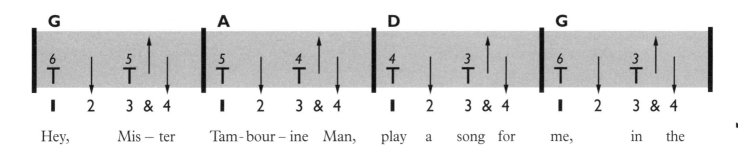

Hey,   Mis – ter   Tam - bour – ine   Man,   play   a   song   for   me,   in   the

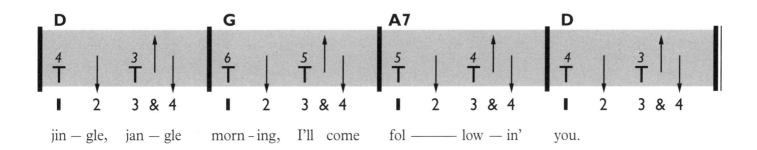

jin – gle,   jan – gle   morn - ing,   I'll   come   fol ——— low — in'   you.

Melody: *To help with your singing, the first notes of the chorus can be found on the 3rd & 2nd frets of the 2nd string.*

Chords: *Notice that the chorus begins with the* **G** *chord (as does the verse). As Bob Dylan does, you can add one or two* **D** *bars before starting the verse. The verse lyrics are at the end of the book.*

Me And Bobby McGee

Kris Kristofferson

Bass-Strum Style

Another Pattern

We're returning to the key of **A** for this great Kris Kristofferson song. I've added another upstrum and some bass variations, but the first note in each bar is always the usual one i.e. 5th for **A**, 6th for **E** and 4th for **D**.

Upstrum Before Chord Change

An upstrum on the offbeat may come just before a chord change. Although the sound is often muffled because the left hand is actually moving when the right hand strikes, the rhythm is kept going.

Don't worry about getting clear notes on strums immediately before a chord change, just make sure your left hand is in the new chord position for the next beat.

Accompaniment: 4/4 Rhythm

Verse

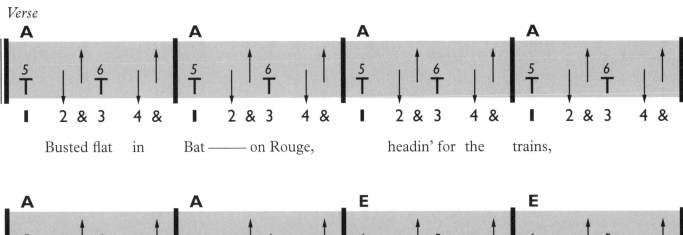

Busted flat in   Bat —— on Rouge,   headin' for the   trains,

feelin' nearly   fad—ed   as   my   jeans.

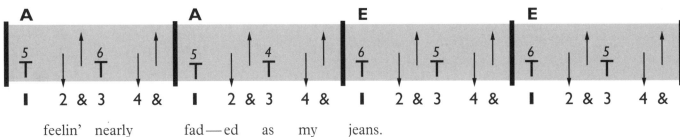

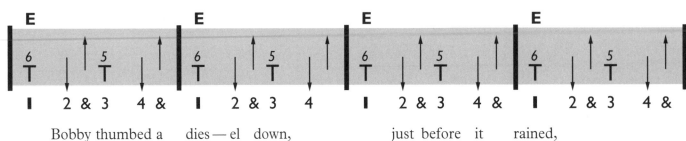

Bobby thumbed a   dies — el   down,   just before   it   rained,

20

Bass-Strum Style

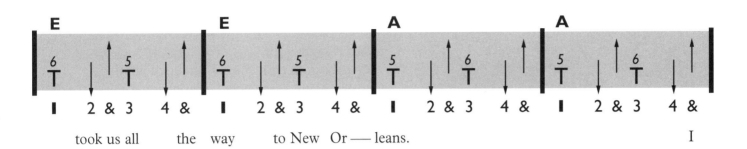

E	E	A	A
6/T	6/T	5/T	5/T
1 2 & 3 4 &	1 2 & 3 4 &	1 2 & 3 4 &	1 2 & 3 4 &

took us all   the   way   to New Or — leans.   I

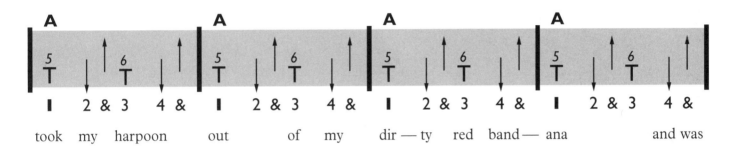

A	A	A	A
5/T 6/T	5/T 6/T	5/T 6/T	5/T 6/T
1 2 & 3 4 &	1 2 & 3 4 &	1 2 & 3 4 &	1 2 & 3 4 &

took   my   harpoon   out   of   my   dir — ty   red   band — ana   and was

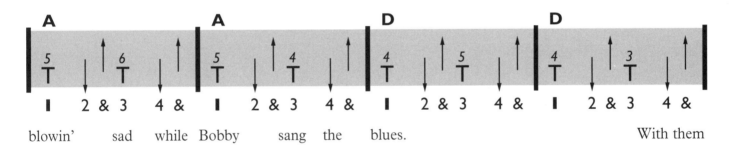

A	A	D	D
5/T 6/T	5/T 4/T	4/T 5/T	4/T 3/T
1 2 & 3 4 &	1 2 & 3 4 &	1 2 & 3 4 &	1 2 & 3 4 &

blowin'   sad   while   Bobby   sang   the   blues.   With them

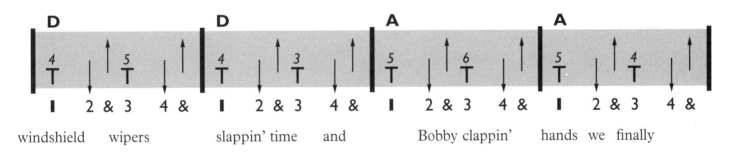

D	D	A	A
4/T 5/T	4/T 3/T	5/T 6/T	5/T 4/T
1 2 & 3 4 &	1 2 & 3 4 &	1 2 & 3 4 &	1 2 & 3 4 &

windshield   wipers   slappin' time   and   Bobby clappin'   hands we finally

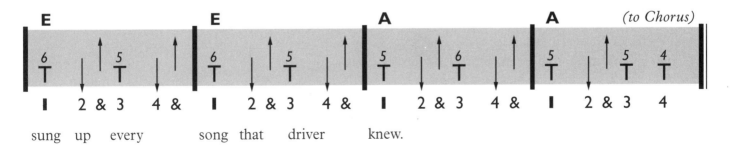

(to Chorus)

E	E	A	A
6/T 5/T	6/T 5/T	5/T 6/T	5/T 5/T 4/T
1 2 & 3 4 &	1 2 & 3 4 &	1 2 & 3 4 &	1 2 & 3 4

sung up every   song that driver   knew.

Notes

The Starting Note *for singing this song can be found on the 2nd fret of the 4th string.*

The Chorus *is given, with chords, at the back of this book.*

Words and Music by Kris Kristofferson and Fred Foster
© 1969 (Renewed 1997) TEMI COMBINE INC.
All Rights Controlled by COMBINE MUSIC CORP. and Administered by EMI BLACKWOOD MUSIC INC.

Love Is All Around

Wet Wet Wet

Bass-Strum Style

Downstrums Between Beats

Like the strumming style, slower songs should sometimes be played with downstrums between beats, instead of upstrums. Here is the same type of pattern that you used for 'Hey Jude', except two single bass notes are struck on the 1st & 3rd beats:

4/4 Rhythm Finger a **D** Chord

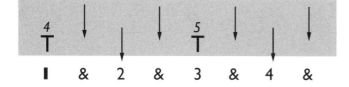

The downstrums between beats should again be played across two or three lower strings. Count the pattern as shown, but the tempo for 'Love Is All Around' should be a little faster than that for 'Hey Jude'. Use the pick if it feels more comfortable for you than thumb and fingers.

Different Patterns

The verse of 'Love Is All Around' has a chord change in each bar, but the pattern still involves single notes on the 1st and 3rd beats. The chorus (shown at the end of the book) has one chord per bar.

You could use one of three possible variations: change the bass note for beat 3; pick out the same bass note on beat 3 as beat 1; or pick out a bass note on beat 1 but not on beat 3. You could even use a strumming pattern without single notes to vary the sound and give the middle section a 'heavier' feel.

Minor Chords

So far you've learned four major chords and two 7 chords. Another kind of chord is often found in accompaniments, the *minor* chord. In the key of **D** you may well come across the **Em** chord, as in 'Love Is All Around.'

Em (E Minor) Chord

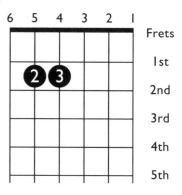

If you hold an **E** chord and remove your 1st finger, it becomes an **Em**. You'll notice that this slight change produces a 'sad' kind of sound, whereas major chords are more upbeat. You can also hold this shape with the 1st & 2nd fingers.

Melody Notes

To help your singing, here's the melody of the first line of lyrics (the second line is the same):

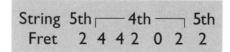

I feel it in my fingers,

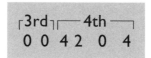

I feel it in my toes.

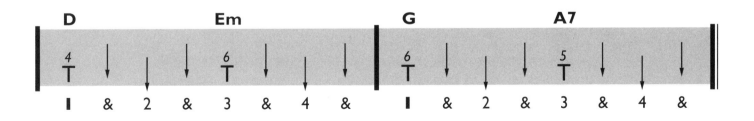

Accompaniment: 4/4 Rhythm

Verse

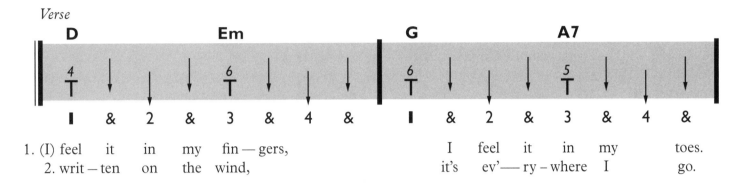

D   Em   G   A7

1 & 2 & 3 & 4 &   1 & 2 & 3 & 4 &

1. (I) feel it in my fin—gers,   I feel it in my toes.
2. writ—ten on the wind,   it's ev'—ry–where I go.

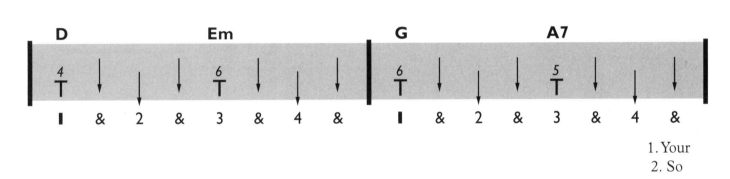

D   Em   G   A7

1 & 2 & 3 & 4 &   1 & 2 & 3 & 4 &

1. Your
2. So

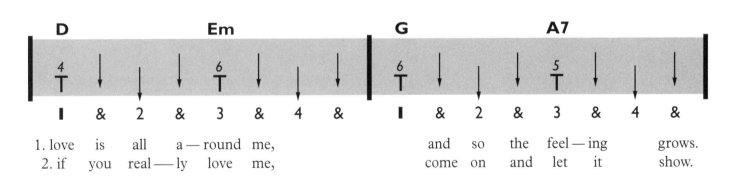

D   Em   G   A7

1 & 2 & 3 & 4 &   1 & 2 & 3 & 4 &

1. love is all a—round me,   and so the feel—ing grows.
2. if you real—ly love me,   come on and let it show.

D   Em   G   A7

1 & 2 & 3 & 4 &   1 & 2 & 3 & 4 &

2. It's

Summary

Now go back to the songs you've played in this section (and then to some of those listed on this page) and try using different patterns.

Bass-Strum Style

Bass-Strum Patterns

A variety of bass-strum patterns are shown below, including the ones you've used for accompaniments already:

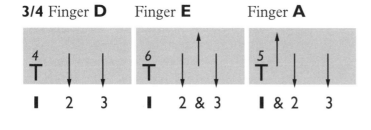

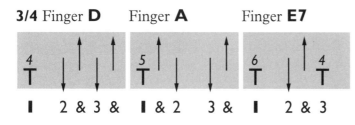

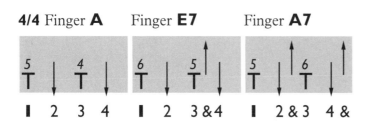

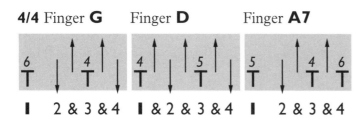

4/4 *(with downstrums between beats)*

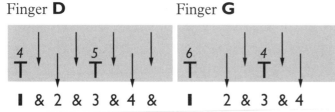

Removing or adding upstrums can change the feel of the rhythm. Experiment with some variations of your own.

Bass-Pluck Style

A very similar style to the bass-strum style is the 'bass-pluck' style, which also uses the bass string strikes as the key feature of the accompaniment. Instead of the strums, you pick all three treble strings together (pluck means an upward pick) with the first three right hand fingers.

The two simple 3/4 and 4/4 patterns work well for this style, and will sound fine for many light and traditional songs.

Other Songs

Here are a few suggestions for songs to play in the bass-strum style, all of which can be played with simple chords:

3/4
Masters Of War
On Top Of Old Smokey
My Bonnie
Liverpool Lou
In Dublin's Fair City
With God On Our Side

4/4
Wild Wood
Ruby Don't Take Your Love To Town
I Walk The Line
This Land Is Your Land
I'm The Urban Spaceman
Colors
The Universal Soldier
Hello Marylou
You're My Best Friend
This Train
It Doesn't Matter Anymore
Rocky Mountain High
Take Me Home Country Roads

4/4 *(with downstrums between beats)*
Hey Joe
Heart Of Gold
Baby I Love Your Way
The Border Song
Mighty Quinn
Oh Danny Boy
A Groovy Kind Of Love

How To Do It

This style of playing involves picking out individual chord notes one after the other by the thumb and three right hand fingers. Try this bar in the 3/4 rhythm:

3/4 Rhythm Finger an **A** Chord

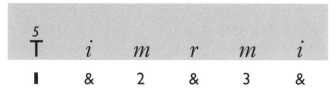

The three right hand fingers are indicated by 'i,' 'm' & 'r' (index, middle and ring fingers).

Here and in the accompaniments that follow, the *index finger always plucks the 3rd string*, the *middle finger always strikes the 2nd string* and the *ring finger always strikes the 1st string*.

As before, the large 'T' and the small number on top of it stand for the thumb strike and which string to play.

Hold your three fingers over the top three treble strings and pluck them in the order shown, after the thumb strike. Don't get the fingers caught under the strings by playing too hard. Make the finger plucks gentle and flowing. Count the pattern as shown. Stress the beat notes more and keep the rhythm steady. Now try a 4/4 pattern:

4/4 Rhythm Finger a **G** Chord

Because the arpeggio style is flowing and continuous, your left hand needs to move quickly to the new position when there is a chord change. If an open bass string note starts the new chord it will be easier, but if it's a fretted note (as in a **G** chord), you must make sure the finger is on the (6th) string in time.

When you can play the 3/4 and 4/4 arpeggio patterns smoothly, you're ready to enjoy some more great songs...

Simple 4/4 Pattern Sequence
Finger an **A** Chord

Thumb strikes 5th string

1st Finger strikes 3rd string

2nd Finger strikes 2nd string

3rd Finger strikes 1st string

Repeat the above sequence to complete a full 4/4 pattern, but start the second half with a 4th string thumb strike.

Scarborough Fair

Traditional, arranged by Russ Shipton

Arpeggio Style

Am and C Chords

Most songs are written in a major key, and the ones you've played so far have all been major. This means the main chord (and the one that the accompaniment will end on) is a major one. Some songs are written in a minor key, where the main chord is minor.

The next song is given in the key of **A** minor. The **Am** chord is shown below, along with another popular chord, **C** major:

Am (A Minor) Chord

C Chord

Although the fingering is quite different between an **A** and an **Am**, notice that there is still just one note changed, and by just one fret.

Helpful Hints

Notice that the bass note changes when another bar of the same chord follows. To start with, you could play the same note again to make things easier. Play the thumb strikes quite hard and make the treble notes softer - your fingers should just brush over the strings.

Near the end of the accompaniment there's a bar of **Em** with just one strum. This helps to create more variety. Play the strum right across all the strings, deliberately and not too fast. Then rest for two beats while singing 'love of.' After that you're back to the usual pattern for two bars of **Am** before beginning the next verse.

Don't forget to experiment with the capo to match your vocal range.

Melody Notes

Here are the melody notes for you to check that you've got the tune right, and for playing along with the accompaniment given. Also, why not try using a strumming pattern against the arpeggio? They should sound pretty good together.

String	⌐3rd⌐	⌐1st⌐	⌐2nd⌐	3rd
Fret	2 2	0 0	0 1	0 2

Are you going to Scarborough Fair?

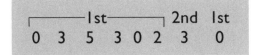

⌐1st⌐	2nd	1st
0 3 5 3 0	2 3	0

Parsley, sage, rosemary and thyme.

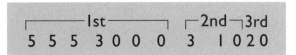

⌐1st⌐	⌐2nd⌐3rd
5 5 5 3 0 0 0	3 1 0 2 0

Remember me to the one who lives there,

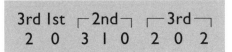

3rd 1st	⌐2nd⌐	⌐3rd⌐
2 0	3 1 0	2 0 2

she once was a true love of mine.

Accompaniment: 3/4 Rhythm

Arpeggio Style

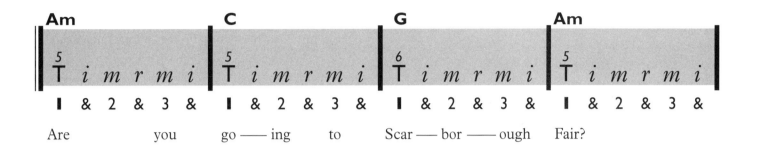

Am   **C**   **G**   **Am**

| $\frac{5}{T}$ i m r m i | $\frac{5}{T}$ i m r m i | $\frac{6}{T}$ i m r m i | $\frac{5}{T}$ i m r m i |
| 1 & 2 & 3 & | 1 & 2 & 3 & | 1 & 2 & 3 & | 1 & 2 & 3 & |

Are   you   go —— ing   to   Scar — bor —— ough   Fair?

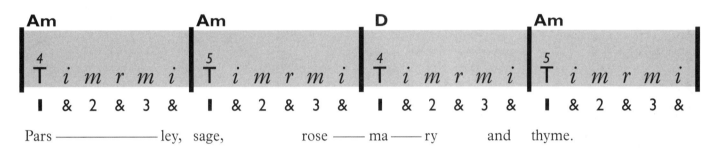

Am   **Am**   **D**   **Am**

| $\frac{4}{T}$ i m r m i | $\frac{5}{T}$ i m r m i | $\frac{4}{T}$ i m r m i | $\frac{5}{T}$ i m r m i |
| 1 & 2 & 3 & | 1 & 2 & 3 & | 1 & 2 & 3 & | 1 & 2 & 3 & |

Pars —————— ley, sage,   rose —— ma —— ry   and   thyme.

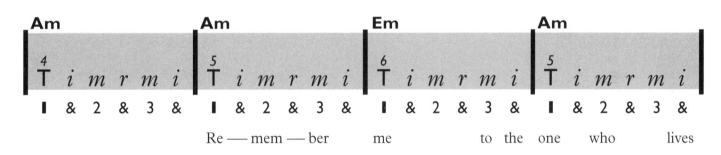

Am   **Am**   **Em**   **Am**

| $\frac{4}{T}$ i m r m i | $\frac{5}{T}$ i m r m i | $\frac{6}{T}$ i m r m i | $\frac{5}{T}$ i m r m i |
| 1 & 2 & 3 & | 1 & 2 & 3 & | 1 & 2 & 3 & | 1 & 2 & 3 & |

Re — mem — ber   me   to the one   who   lives

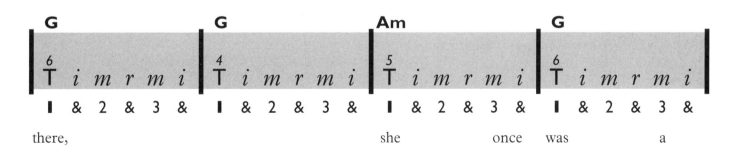

G   **G**   **Am**   **G**

| $\frac{6}{T}$ i m r m i | $\frac{4}{T}$ i m r m i | $\frac{5}{T}$ i m r m i | $\frac{6}{T}$ i m r m i |
| 1 & 2 & 3 & | 1 & 2 & 3 & | 1 & 2 & 3 & | 1 & 2 & 3 & |

there,   she   once   was   a

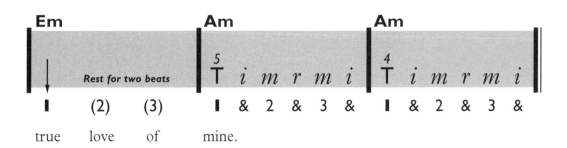

Em   **Am**   **Am**

| ↓   *Rest for two beats* | $\frac{5}{T}$ i m r m i | $\frac{4}{T}$ i m r m i |
| 1   (2)   (3) | 1 & 2 & 3 & | 1 & 2 & 3 & |

true   love   of   mine.

Why Worry

Dire Straits

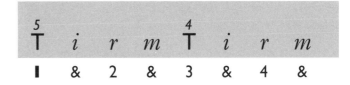

Arpeggio Style

B7 Chord

You've used two major keys so far, **A** & **D**. This next accompaniment is written in another popular guitar key, the key of **E** major. The three main chords in this key are **E**, **A** & **B**, but because the **B** chord is hard to finger many guitarists prefer to use the **B7** chord instead:

B7 Chord

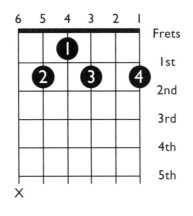

All four fingers are used for the **B7**. The 2nd string is played open but the 6th string shouldn't be sounded.

Alternative Patterns

When you've mastered the accompaniment on the next page, try changing the order of the treble strings and maybe mixing the patterns up for variety and different effects. Here are two possibilities, try inventing some of your own:

4/4 Rhythm Finger an **E** Chord

6				4			
T	r	m	i	T	r	m	i
1	&	2	&	3	&	4	&

4/4 Rhythm Finger a **B7** Chord

5				4			
T	i	r	m	T	i	r	m
1	&	2	&	3	&	4	&

Remember that the index finger always strikes the 3rd string, the middle finger the 2nd string and the 3rd finger the top string.

Alternative Styles

Many songs sound better if they're played in a particular style. Often that will mean the way they were arranged by the original writer. Sometimes though, it might be worth experimenting with different styles to see what they sound like for the same song.

In the classroom, different groups can play alternative styles at the same time. At home you could do the same thing by playing along with a recording or a friend.

Melody Notes

The chorus of 'Why Worry' is given on the next page. Here are the melody notes:

String	⌐3rd⌐	4th	⌐— 3rd —⌐	⌐— 4th —⌐	3rd
Fret	2 1	2	2 2 2	4 4	2 4 1

Why worry, there should be laughter after pain,

	⌐— 3rd —⌐	⌐ 4th ⌐	3rd
2	2 2 1	4 2	4 1

there should be sunshine after rain.

	⌐— 3rd —⌐	⌐— 4th —	3rd
2	2 2 1	4 2	4 1

These things have always been the same,

4th	⌐3rd⌐	4th	⌐3rd⌐	4th
4	2 1	1 2	2 1	1 2

so why worry now, why worry now?

Accompaniment: 4/4 Rhythm

Chorus

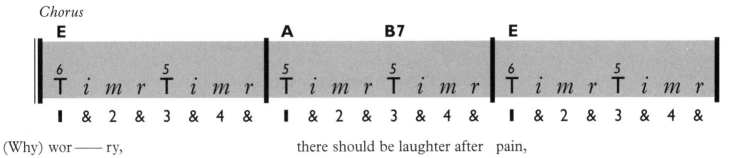

(Why) wor —— ry,   there should be laughter after   pain,

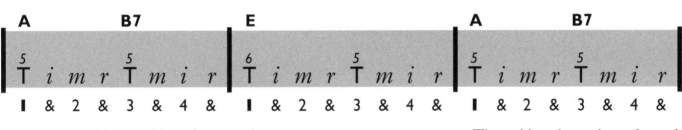

there should be sunshine after   rain.   These things have always been the

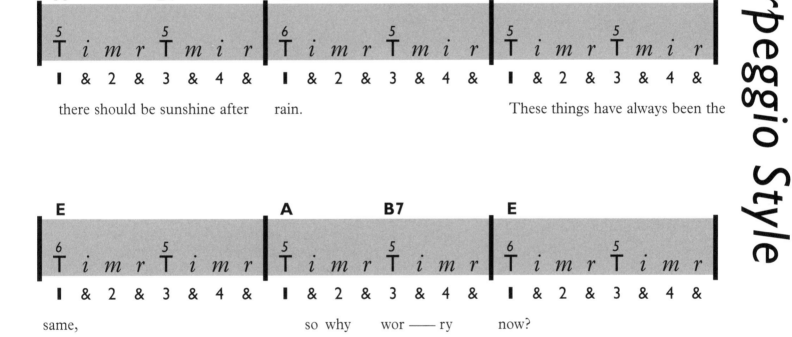

same,   so why   wor —— ry   now?

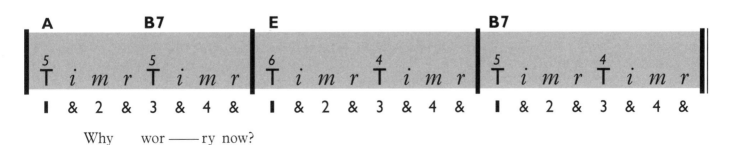

Why   wor ——ry now?

Verses: *The verses of 'Why Worry' are given at the back of this book.*

Arpeggio Style

Words and Music by Mark Knopfler

Wonderful Tonight

Eric Clapton

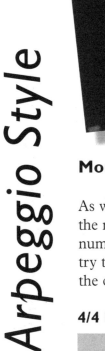

The Key Of G Major

Another popular guitar key is **G** Major. This is the key that Eric Clapton uses to play the song himself. The main chords are **G**, **C** & **D**. The **Em** chord often occurs in the key of **G** Major (as well as **D** Major, where you saw it).

Melody Notes

Here are the notes to help you sing the verse of 'Wonderful Tonight':

String	4th	⌐2nd⌐	3rd	2nd	3rd	⌐2nd⌐	
Fret	0	0	1	0	2	3	0	1	1

It's late in the evening, she's wond'rin

⌐2nd⌐	⌐3rd⌐	4th	⌐2nd⌐	3rd	2nd
0	0	2	2	0	0	1	0	2	3

what clothes to wear. She puts on her make-up,

3rd	⌐2nd⌐	⌐3rd⌐
0	0	1	0	0	2	2

and brushes her long, blonde hair.

⌐1st⌐	2nd	3rd	⌐2nd⌐	3rd
0	0	0	3	2	0	0	0	3	0

And then she asks me, "Do I look all right?"

⌐3rd⌐	2nd	⌐3rd⌐	4th	3rd
0	2	0	1	1	0	2	2	0	0	0

And I say "Yes, you look wonderful tonight."

The middle section chords are shown with all the song lyrics at the end of the book.

More Patterns

As well as switching the order of the treble strings, the rhythmic feel can be altered by changing the number and position of the thumb strikes. You could try this pattern for 'Wonderful Tonight' instead of the one shown:

4/4 Rhythm Finger a **G** Chord

T	i	m	r	m	i	T	i
6						5	

| 1 | & | 2 | & | 3 | & | 4 | & |

Accompaniment: 4/4 Rhythm

Verse

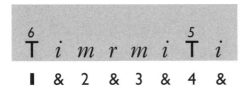

G								**D**								**C**							
T	i	m	i	r	m	i	m	T	i	m	i	r	m	i	m	T	i	m	i	r	m	i	m
6								4								5							

| 1 | & | 2 | & | 3 | & | 4 | & | 1 | & | 2 | & | 3 | & | 4 | & | 1 | & | 2 | & | 3 | & | 4 | & |

It's late in the   eve — ning,   she's wondering what

T	= Thumb
i	= Index finger
m	= Middle finger
r	= Ring finger

Arpeggio Style

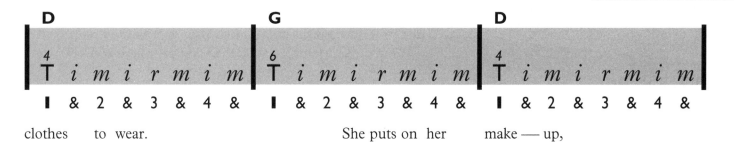

clothes   to wear.   She puts on her   make — up,

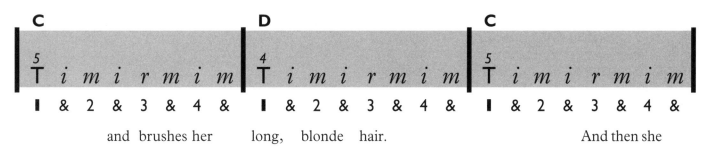

                and brushes her   long, blonde   hair.   And then she

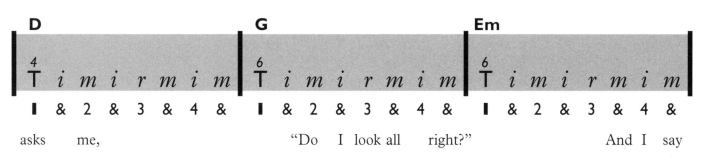

asks   me,   "Do   I look all   right?"   And I   say

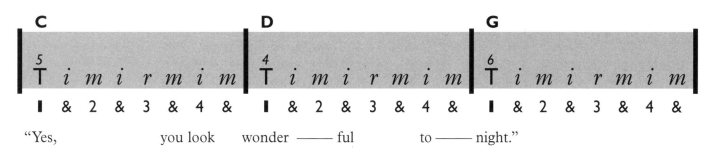

"Yes,   you look   wonder —— ful   to —— night."

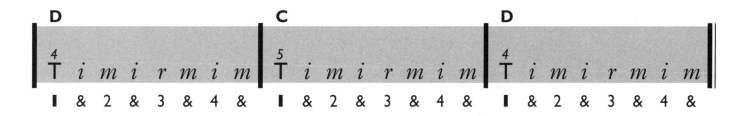

Words and Music by Eric Clapton

Summary

Arpeggio Patterns

A variety of arpeggio patterns are shown below, including those you've already used in this section:

3/4 Finger **Am**

5					
T	*i*	*m*	*r*	*m*	*i*
1	&	2	&	3	&

Finger **G**

6					
T	*r*	*m*	*i*	*m*	*r*
1	&	2	&	3	&

3/4 Finger **E**

6					
T	*i*	*m*	*i*	*r*	*m*
1	&	2	&	3	&

Finger **B7**

5				4	
T	*i*	*m*	*r*	T	*i*
1	&	2	&	3	&

4/4 Finger **E**

6				5			
T	*i*	*m*	*r*	T	*i*	*m*	*r*
1	&	2	&	3	&	4	&

Finger **B7**

5				4			
T	*i*	*r*	*m*	T	*i*	*r*	*m*
1	&	2	&	3	&	4	&

4/4 Finger **D**

4							
T	*i*	*m*	*r*	*m*	*r*	*m*	*i*
1	&	2	&	3	&	4	&

Finger **Am**

5							
T	*i*	*m*	*i*	*r*	*m*	*i*	*m*
1	&	2	&	3	&	4	&

4/4 Finger **C**

5						4	
T	*i*	*m*	*r*	*m*	*i*	T	*i*
1	&	2	&	3	&	4	&

Finger **Em**

6				5		4	
T	*r*	*m*	*i*	T	*i*	T	*i*
1	&	2	&	3	&	4	&

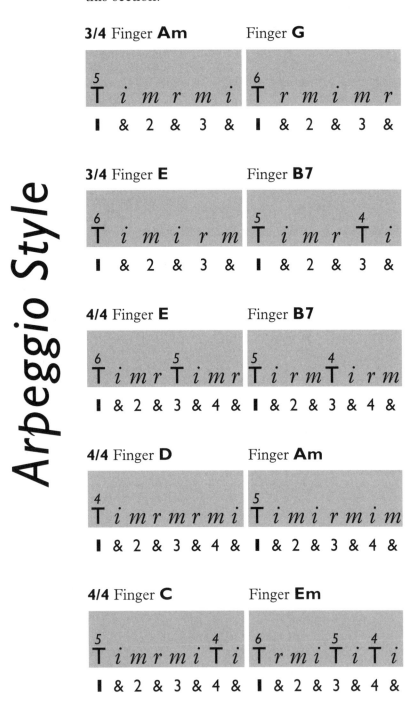

Changing the order of the fingers and the number of bass strikes can alter the feel of the rhythm. Experiment with some variations of your own.

Now go back to the songs you've played in this section (and then to some of those listed on this page) and try using different patterns.

Other Songs

Many slower, ballad-type songs are suited to the arpeggio style. You're sure to recognize some of the songs listed below, all of which can be played with simple chords and will sound great with an arpeggio accompaniment.

3/4
Bird On A Wire
Lavender's Blue
Around The World
When Two Worlds Collide
Mistletoe And Wine
Sisters Of Mercy
Joan Of Arc
Amazing Grace

4/4
The Rose
Turn, Turn, Turn
Wild Mountain Thyme
Where Have All The Flowers Gone
Hey, That's No Way To Say Goodbye
From Both Sides Now
The Sound Of Silence
The Leaving Of Liverpool
Carrickfergus
English Country Garden
A Little Peace
Green Green Grass Of Home
A Groovy Kind Of Love

Mull Of Kintyre

Verse 1

A   A   A   A
Far have I travelled and much have I seen
D   D   A   A
Dark distant mountains with valleys of green
A   A   A   A
Past painted deserts, the sunset's on fire
**   D   D   E   A A**
As he carries me home to the Mull of Kintyre.

Chorus
Mull of Kintyre, oh mist rolling in from the sea
My desire is always to be here, oh Mull of Kintyre.

Verse 2
Sweep through the heather like deer in the glen
Oh carry me back to the days I knew then
Nights when we sang like a heavenly choir
Of the life and the times of the Mull of Kintyre

Verse 3
Smiles in the sunshine and tears in the rain
Still take me back where my memories remain
Flickering embers grow higher and higher
As they carry me back to the Mull of Kintyre.

The Times They Are A-Changin'

Verse 1
Come gather round people, wherever you roam
And admit that the waters around you have grown
And accept it that soon you'll be drenched to the bone
If your time to you is worth savin'
Then you'd better start swimmin' or you'll sink
     like a stone
For the times they are a-changin'.

Verse 2
Come writers and critics who prophesize with your pen
And keep your eyes wide, the chance won't come again
And don't speak too soon for the wheel's still in spin
And there's no tellin' who that it's namin'
For the loser now will be later to win
For the times they are a-changin'.

Verse 3
Come senators, congressmen, please heed the call
Don't stand in the doorway, don't block up the hall
For he that gets hurt will be he who has stalled
There's a battle outside ragin'
It'll soon shake your windows and rattle your walls
For the times they are a-changin'.

Verse 4
Come mothers and fathers throughout the land
And don't criticize what you can't understand
Your sons and your daughters are beyond
     your command
Your old road is rapidly agin'
Please get out of the new one if you can't lend
     your hand
For the times they are a-changin'.

Verse 5
The line it is drawn, the curse it is cast
The slow one now will later be fast
As the present now will later be past
The order is rapidly fadin'
And the first one now will later be last
For the times they are a-changin'.

Candle In The Wind

Verse 1

     A   A   D

Goodbye Norma Jean, though I never knew you

     D

   at all

                    A   A

You had the grace to hold yourself, while those

          D   D

  around you crawled

                  A A

They crawled out of the woodwork, and they

          D   D

  whispered into your brain

               A   A

They set you on a treadmill and they made you

          D

  change your name.

Chorus

And it seems to me you lived your life like a candle
   in the wind
Never knowing who to cling to when the rain set in
And I would have liked to have known you, but
   I was just a kid
Your candle burnt out long before your legend ever did.

Verse 2

Loneliness was tough, the toughest role you
   ever played
Hollywood created a superstar and pain was the
   price you paid
Even when you died the press still hounded you
All the papers had to say was that Marilyn was found in
   the nude.

Verse 3

Goodbye Norma Jean, though I never knew
   you at all
You had the grace to hold yourself while those
   around you crawled
Goodbye Norma Jean, from the young man in
   the twenty-second row
Who sees you as something more than sexual,
   more than just our Marilyn Monroe.

Blowin' In The Wind

Verse 1

How many roads must a man walk down
Before you call him a man?
How many seas must the white dove sail
Before she sleeps in the sand?
Yes'n how many times must the cannon balls fly
Before they're forever banned?

Chorus

The answer, my friend, is blowin' in the wind
The answer is blowin' in the wind.

Verse 2

Yes'n how many years can a mountain exist
Before it is washed to the sea?
Yes'n how many years can some people exist
Before they're allowed to be free?
Yes'n how many times can a man turn his head
And pretend that he just doesn't see?

Verse 3

Yes'n how many times must a man look up
Before he can see the sky?
Yes'n how many ears must one man have
Before he can hear people cry?
Yes'n how many deaths will it take till he knows
That too many people have died?

Hey Jude

Verse 1
Hey Jude, don't make it bad
Take a sad song and make it better
Remember to let her into your heart
Then you can start to make it better.

Verse 2
Hey Jude, don't be afraid
You were made to go out and get her
The minute you let her under your skin
Then you begin to make it better.

Middle Section
A (A7)   **D**   **D**
And any time you feel the pain, hey Jude, refrain
          E   **A**   **A (A7)**
Don't carry the world upon your shoulders
             D   **D**
For well you know that it's a fool who plays it cool
      E   **A**
By making his world a little colder
    A   **E**   **E (E7)**
Na na na na-na, na na na na.

Verse 3
Hey Jude, don't let me down
You have found her, now go and get her
Remember to let her into your heart
Then you can start to make it better.

Middle Section 2
So let it out and let it in
Hey Jude, begin
You're waiting for someone to perform with
And don't you know that it's just you
Hey Jude, you'll do
The movement you need is on your shoulders.
Na na na na-na, na na na na.

Verse 4
Hey Jude, don't make it bad
Take a sad song and make it better
Remember to let her under your skin
Then you'll begin to make it better.

Better, better, better, better, better, oh...

Na, na, na, na na na na... na na na na...
Hey Jude.

Catch The Wind

Verse 1
In the chilly hours and minutes of uncertainty
I want to be in the warm hold of your lovin' mind
To feel you all around me and to take your hand
    along the sand
Ah, but I may as well try and catch the wind.

Verse 2
When sundown pales the sky
I want to hide a while behind your smile
And everywhere I'd look your eyes I'd find
For me to love you now would be the sweetest thing
    it would make me sing
Ah, but I may as well try and catch the wind.

Verse 3
When rain has hung the leaves with tears
I want you near to kill my fears
To help me to leave all my blues behind
For standin' in your heart is where I want to be and
    I long to be
Ah, but I may as well try and catch the wind.

Mr. Tambourine Man

Verse 1

        G   **A**   **D**
Though I know that evening's empire has returned
        G
   into sand
D   **G**   **D**   **G**
Vanished from my hand, left me blindly here to stand
         A   **A**
But still not sleepin'
        G   **A**   **D**   **G**
My weariness amazes me, I'm branded on my feet
  D   **G**   **D**   **G**
I have no one to meet, and the ancient, empty street's
         A   **A**
  too dead for dreamin.'

Chorus
Hey, Mister Tambourine Man, play a song for me
I'm not sleepy and there is no place I'm goin' to
Hey, Mister Tambourine Man, play a song for me
In the jingle, jangle morning I'll come followin' you.

Verse 2
Take me on a trip upon your magic, swirlin' ship
My senses have been stripped, my hands can't
    feel to grip
My toes too numb to step, wait only for my boot
    heels to be wanderin'
I'm ready to go anywhere, I'm ready for to fade
Into my own parade, cast your dancin' spell my way
I promise to go under it.

Verse 3
Though you might hear laughin', spinnin', swingin'
Madly across the sun, it's not aimed at anyone
It's just escapin' on the run, and but for the sky
    there are no fences facin'
And if you hear vague traces of skippin' reels of rhyme
To your tambourine in time, it's just a ragged
    clown behind
I wouldn't pay it any mind, it's just a shadow
    you're seein' that he's chasin'.

Verse 4
Then take me disappearin' through the smoke
    rings of my mind
Down the foggy ruins of time, far past the frozen leaves
The haunted, frightened trees, out to the windy beach
Far from the twisted reach of crazy sorrow
Yes, to dance beneath the diamond sky with one
    hand wavin' free
Silhouetted by the sea, circled by the circus sands
With all memory and fate driven deep beneath
    the waves
Let me forget about today until tomorrow.

Lyrics

Me And Bobby McGee

Verse 1
Busted flat in Baton Rouge, headin' for the trains
Feelin' nearly faded as my jeans
Bobby thumbed a diesel down, just before it rained
Took us all the way to New Orleans
I pulled my harpoon out of my dirty red bandana
And was blowin' sad while Bobby sang the blues
With them windshield wipers slappin' time
And Bobby clappin' hands
We finally sang up every song that driver knew.

Chorus 1
   D   **D**   **A**   **A**
Freedom's just another word for nothin' left to lose
     E   **E**   **A** **A(A7)**
And nothin' ain't worth nothin', but it's free
   D   **D**   **A**
Feelin' good was easy, Lord, when Bobby sang the blues
   E   **E**   **E E**
Feelin' good was good enough for me
 E (E7)   **E (E7)**   **A** **A**
Good enough for me and Bobby McGee.

Verse 2
From the coalmines of Kentucky, to the California sun
Bobby shared the secrets of my soul
Standin' right beside me through everything I done
And every night she kept me from the cold
Then somewhere near Salinas, Lord, I let her slip away
Lookin' for the home I hoped she'd find
Well, I'd trade all my tomorrows for a single yesterday
Holdin' Bobby's body next to mine.

Love Is All Around

Verse 1
I feel it in my fingers, I feel it in my toes
Your love is all around me, and so the feeling grows
It's written on the wind, it's everywhere I go
So if you really love me, come on and let it show.

Chorus
     G   **Em**
You know I love you, I always will
G   **D**
My mind's made up by the way that I feel
     G   **Em**
There's no beginning, there'll be no end
   Em   **A**
'Cause on my love you can depend.

Verse 2
I see your face before me, as I lay on my bed
I kinda get to thinkin' of all the things you said
You gave your promise to me, and I gave mine to you
I need someone beside me in everything I do.

Scarborough Fair

Verse 1
Are you goin' to Scarborough Fair
Parsley, sage, rosemary and thyme
Remember me to one who lives there
She once was a true love of mine.

Verse 2
Tell her to make me a cambric shirt
Parsley, sage, rosemary and thyme
Without any seam or needle work
Then she'll be a true love of mine.

Verse 3
Tell her to find me an acre of land
Parsley, sage, rosemary and thyme
Between the salt water and the sea strand
Then she'll be a true love of mine.

Verse 4
Tell her to plough it with a sickle of leather
Parsley, sage, rosemary and thyme
And bind it all in a bunch of heather
Then she'll be a true love of mine.

Why Worry

Verse 1

E B7   **E B7**
Baby, I see this world has made you sad
                 E   A
Some people can be bad
            (F♯)   **B7 B7**
The things they do, the things they say
       E B7   **E   B7**
But baby, I'll wipe away those bitter tears
                    E   A
I'll chase away those restless fears
            (F♯)   **B7 B7**
That turn your blue skies into grey.

Chorus
Why worry, there should be laughter after pain
There should be sunshine after rain
These things have always been the same
So why worry now, why worry now?

Verse 2
Baby, when I get down I turn to you
And you make sense of what I do
I know it isn't hard to say
But baby, just when this world seems mean and cold
Our love comes shining red and gold
And all the rest is by the way.

Wonderful Tonight

Verse 1
It's late in the evening, she's wonderin' what
    clothes to wear
She puts on her make-up and brushes her long,
    blonde hair
And then she asks me, "Do I look all right?"
And I say, "Yes, you look wonderful tonight."

Verse 2
We go to a party, and everyone turns to see
This beautiful lady, who's walking around with me
And then she asks me, "Do you feel all right?"
And I say, "Yes, I feel wonderful tonight."

Middle Section
          C   **D**   **G**   **Em**
I feel wonderful because I see the love light in your eyes
          C   **D**   **C**   **D**
And the wonder of it all is that you just don't realize
          G
How much I love you.

Verse 3
It's time to go home now, and I've got an achin' head
So I give her the car keys and she helps me to bed
And then I tell her, as I turn out the light
I say, "My darling, you were wonderful tonight."

About The Capo

Most acoustic (and many electric) guitarists use this important device. The capo shortens the guitar strings and increases their pitch by the same amount. It can be placed on any fret (just behind the fret wire).

Using The Capo

To be effective, the capo must press all the strings down firmly. The first capo (pictured below) simply clamps across the strings, like a very strong clip or peg. (Here, it is shown on the third fret). The second type (below left) involves a screw which is adjusted so a rubber covered bar is firmly clamped across the strings.

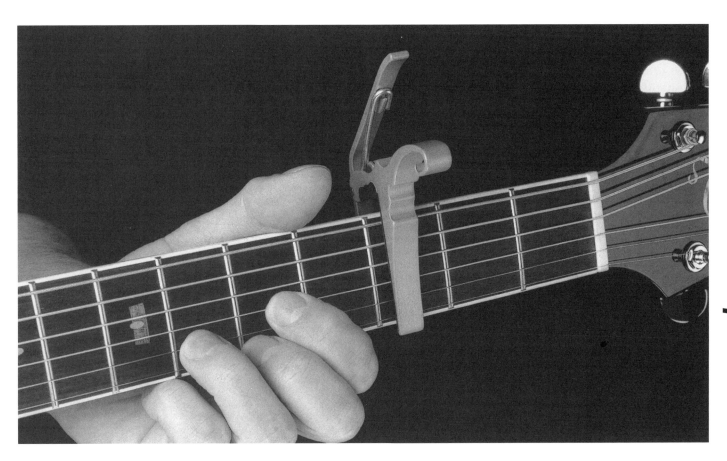

If the pitch of a song doesn't suit your vocal range, the capo can be put somewhere on the neck of the guitar. The position of the capo can be changed until the melody suits your voice. The same chord shapes can be played as before, but singing will be easier.

One person can play without a capo and use one group of chord shapes, while another can put a capo on and play a different group of chord shapes. They can sound great when played together. Try these two possibilities:-

1st Player (or group)
Chords **A**, **D** and **E** (no capo)
2nd Player (or group)
Chord shapes **D**, **G** and **A** (capo on 7th fret)

1st Player (or group)
Chords **D**, **G** and **A** (no capo)
2nd Player (or group)
Chord shapes **A**, **D** and **E** (capo on 5th fret)

The Capo

Closing Comments

Congratulations!

You've reached the end of the first book. You're no longer a beginner and the hardest part is over.

Now you know ten chords and various patterns in three quite different right hand styles. This is a good basis for developing a broad ability in guitar playing.

Some of you may have been playing the guitar for a while before using this book, so you may have found it easier than others, but there's always something to gain from any new material. Don't pass over things too quickly. You might not know them as well as you think.

In the 2nd and 3rd books I'll gradually explain more music theory, and introduce some classical pieces, so you can see how the different types of music are related.

Those of you who have already studied some music theory should try to tie in your knowledge with what you've been playing on the guitar. A little musical knowledge helps greatly in arranging material quickly and increasing your repertoire.

Before going on to the next book, try to find some songs that can be played with the chords you know, and experiment with the various right hand styles and patterns. Then I want you to remember the open string notes of the guitar:

e	a	d	g	b	e	Notes
6	5	4	3	2	1	String Numbers

Frets

1st
2nd
3rd
4th
5th

Have you committed the open string notes to memory? Good - see you in Book Two, for more great songs and interesting things to learn!

Exclusive distributors:
Music Sales Corporation
257 Park Avenue South, New York, NY 10010 USA.
Music Sales Limited
8/9 Frith Street, London W1D 3JB, England.
Music Sales Pty Limited
120 Rothschild Avenue, Rosebery,
NSW 2018, Australia.

Order No. AM 973797
ISBN 0.8256.1933.5
This book © Copyright 2002 by Amsco Publications.

Unauthorized reproduction of any part of this publication by any means including photocopying is an infringement of copyright.

Written and arranged by Russ Shipton.
Edited by Sorcha Armstrong.
Cover and book design by Michael Bell Design.
Cover and guitar photography by George Taylor.
Guitars supplied by Rhodes Music.
Artist photographs courtesy of
    London Features International and Retna.
Printed in the United States of America by
    Vicks Lithograph and Printing Corporation.

CD programmed by John Moores.
All guitars by Arthur Dick.
Engineered by Kester Sims.

www.musicsales.com